THE VIKINGS

©

C. A. Burland

1959

First published 1959 by

HULTON EDUCATIONAL PUBLICATIONS LTD.

161-166, Fleet Street, London, E.C.4

Printed in Great Britain by

Hills & Lacy Limited

Watford, Hertfordshire

THE
VIKINGS

by

C. A. BURLAND

Illustrated by

R. G. BOTTING, A.R.C.A

HULTON EDUCATIONAL PUBLICATIONS

CONTENTS

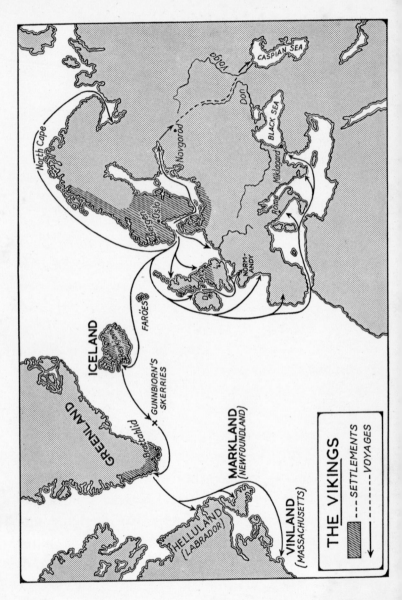

THE VIKINGS

SETTLEMENTS ----
VOYAGES -----

CASPIAN SEA

Volga

Don

BLACK SEA

Rome

Miklagard

North Cape

Novgorod

Bergen

Oslo

NORM-
ANDY

FARÖES

ICELAND

Reykjavik

GREENLAND

Brattahlid

× GUNNBIORN'S SKERRIES

MARKLAND
(NEWFOUNDLAND)

HELLULAND
(LABRADOR)

VINLAND
(MASSACHUSETTS)

The Viking Homeland

The Vikings (they pronounced it Vik-ings, and not Vi-kings) were the people who lived on the *viks*, the little sea inlets which spread along the coasts of Norway, south Sweden and Denmark. Their homeland was covered in pine forests. Norway consisted mainly of the narrow fiords penetrating among forest-covered mountains coming right down to the sea. Only in southern Sweden were there inland rivers of any importance, so most of the Vikings were dwellers near the sea. There were tracks through the forests fit for a file of horsemen to travel, but they were neither easy nor safe. It was much better to travel by ship. To most of the Viking farmers the sea was a great roadway. They called it by many names, like the Ships' Path, the Swan Road, the Whale's Bath.

Their farms were meadowland cleared from the forests. Here they kept sheep, goats and cattle, and grew crops of rye and barley. They had few towns of any size, mostly because they hated living cramped together. They did not like anything that interfered with their freedom. So, when King Harald Hardrada united Norway in 872, many free farmers left to find new lands to settle in, rather than submit to an overlord.

Where the Vikings Travelled

In early days the farmers would take ship just as you might take your bicycle to visit friends and relatives. But, later on in the tenth century, when the changes at home made many men seek adventure elsewhere, they took their ships further afield. Some came to Scotland and Ireland, where they fought and founded little kingdoms of their own in the Orkneys and Hebrides, and around Dublin in Ireland. They captured the Isle of Man and raided the coasts of England.

Others went further afield, discovered Iceland and settled there. From Iceland, Erik the Red was outlawed and spent his three years of exile in discovering Greenland. Later he returned there and set up as a farmer and fisherman. One of his sons, Leif the Lucky, discovered North America. For a few years Vikings settled on the New England Coast of the United States. But the Indians killed off the cattle in a war, and the Viking settlers decided to return to Greenland.

Some Viking nobles travelled south-eastwards with their followers and formed the Varangian Guard of the Emperors of Constantinople. Their name simply means ''Far Rangers''. The chieftain, Rurik, set out to follow the rivers of Europe and founded a government at Novgorod in Russia. Some of his followers went down the Volga as far as the Caspian Sea. Another nobleman, Rolf Ganger, raided France and set up the Duchy of Normandy. (His name means "The Walker", because he had such long legs that when he rode a pony his feet touched the ground.)

Still others fought in North-East England. You will know that King Alfred was successful in forcing them back to the northern half of the kingdom when he defeated them at the battle of Essandun.

It is rather funny to think that the Vikings first started raiding and fighting to escape from being subjects of a king; but all the countries where they settled became kingdoms.

A Skuta (small fast ship) coming to anchor in the Vik

In England they eventually became subjects of the greatest of all their own kings, Canute.

The Farms

Beside the vik there was usually a cosy little homestead, with fields around the cluster of farm buildings. They

A Viking farmstead with its wooden palisades

Inside the great timber farmhouse

were built at some place where it was easy to get down to the sea. The houses were on a piece of rising ground where they could be defended in case of need. The farmhouse was rather like a great, low, wooden barn. The floor was of beaten earth, sometimes lined with slabs of stone. The walls were made of split tree trunks set side by side in a double layer, standing upright. The roof was supported on big wooden beams. It sloped sharply and was covered with wooden shingles. Some houses had thatched roofs. One end was the hall where the

15

The fireplace and cauldron of stew in the middle of the hall

people sat, and talked, and ate their meals. The bed-rooms were closed chambers in the hall. Across the middle of the house came a wooden screen and the side doorway. The other half of the building housed the stalls for the cattle.

On the floor in the middle of the hall was a fire of wood. The smoke went up among the rafters and even-

16

tually escaped through a hole in the smoke-blackened roof.

~~~~~~

Furniture

~~~~~~

The screens in a rich house, and particularly the door posts, were carved and painted with interlacing designs of dragons and warriors. Along each side of the hall were plain wooden tables with well-scrubbed tops, and beside them were wooden benches. At the head of the hall was a cross table where the head of the household sat with his wife. If they were rich people they might have seats with backs and arms. A nobleman thought that his seat posts were sacred things. They were richly carved and some-times decorated with real gold leaf. When the first Viking sett-lers reached Iceland their leader threw his seat posts into the sea, and claimed the land nearest to where they were washed up. To him they were

A chieftain's seat post

B

Wooden bucket for water

the signs of his power, and of his good luck.

Around the fire were iron bars to keep the logs in place, and over it hung a cauldron of stew always kept hot.

On the floor were clean rushes or sometimes soft layers of pine needles; but that was on the side where the benches were, not in the middle near the fire. Wooden houses might be set on fire too easily, so no one took risks.

There were wooden buckets and tubs, with fine iron and bronze hoops and handles. These held water, beer, honey, butter and such good things for food. The coarse brown bread was made in rings and hung on ropes.

Two grey pottery vases and a glass beaker

18

Pottery was black or grey and very simple, just bowls, jugs and beakers. Plates of wood were used instead of china plates. Rich houses had some wall hangings of coloured cloth, but that was a luxury which few people could afford. But there were plenty of skins to make seats softer. Beds were boxes lined with sweet-scented hay in which one lay wrapped up in a woollen coverlet.

Farm Buildings

The cattle byre was often part of the main house, but separate from where the people lived. The cattle were kept in their stalls. There was straw for them to lie on, and mangers for hay and troughs for water. In the long winters the Viking farmer kept only enough cattle to fill his byre. The others were killed in the autumn. Their flesh was salted down in barrels, to be eaten during the winter.

There was a dairy where the women of the house took the milk and churned it by hand, shaking and

Woman churning butter

The cowherd brings water for the cattle

rocking the churn until the yellow butter-fat separated. The butter-milk left behind was sweet and pleasant to drink. It was given to the children. Some milk was soured, and the curd separated. This was squeezed in cloth bags in wooden presses until it had turned into a hard white cheese, which was well salted and would keep for months.

Usually a farm had a separate, rougher house for the servants and serfs, and a fine stable for the horses.

Horses were for riding, not for farm work. They were a sign that a householder was of good family, and they were thought to be sacred to the god Odin. There was a separate workshop for woodwork. Some people had a blacksmith's workshop for making farm tools, horse-shoes and weapons.

So, you see, each farm was a little village in itself.

A young nobleman and his horse

The Temple

Each farmstead had its sacred place. Usually this was a circular wooden building inside a wooden fence. Within it were simple wooden images of the gods. Each head of a family was his own priest and had to lead the worship of the gods. If he made any mistake in his prayers, or in

The wooden temple of Odin and the Norse gods

the way he moved in the temple—he must always walk round the way of the sun—he would bring bad luck to all the family. It was in the temple that the Godi, as he was called, would call on the gods to help the fields to be fruitful. He would offer them a share of the food of the household, and talk to them as if they were wise elder brothers who would help him. If he had enemies he wished to harm, he would sing charms and magic spells to hurt them. For great religious ceremonies he would go on pilgrimage to some more famous sacred spot where priests would lead ceremonies. These men knew how to read and write. They used signs called runes. Most people knew a few of these letters, but very few could use them properly for writing. They thought them to be a great magic given to them by Odin, who stole them from the giant, Mimir.

Iron Workers

People who worked in iron were specialists with a secret knowledge of their own. They often earned enough to become rich landowners. Most of them, however, worked for the farmers and lived with the family. Their craft always made them rather special persons. Most of them bought their iron, in bars brought by trading ships.

Furnace for heating iron

The rough iron was heated up in a fire of charcoal, pumped by a big leather bellows. When it was bright cherry red it was beaten out on a stone anvil. Usually the hammers were made of iron, but some people preferred to use stone hammers for the work. Before making anything, the iron was beaten out, and then bent over double, heated nearly white hot, and hammered together just before it began to melt, and so on, over and over again. In

Viking weapons

24

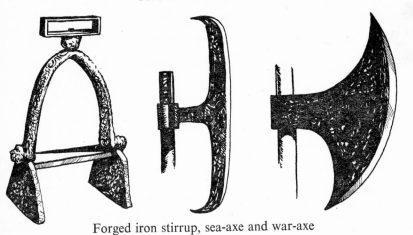

Forged iron stirrup, sea-axe and war-axe

this way impurities were beaten out of the metal, and it was made more even, all the way through. Such wrought iron was used for making ploughshares, horse-shoes and axe-blades for the farm.

Weapons were more carefully made. The iron was made very pure by beating and reheating, and then strips of iron from different bars were heated up and plaited together while they were soft. Some swordsmiths even knotted their strips of iron. Then the whole piece was made white hot and welded by hammering. Such weapons had a kind of ornamental wavy grain from the different pieces of iron showing all over them. They were very handsome, and had a keen cutting edge. Very clever smiths knew how to cut out spaces in the iron blades and inlay them with pieces of silver and gold. Some-

25

times these inlays spelled out the name of the owner, or even some lucky charm, in letters of the Runic alphabet. No wonder the warriors thought them magic weapons!

Wood Workers

Almost all Vikings could carve well. In the long winter evenings they loved to carve a block of wood with adzes, chisels and sharp knives. They were experts in the use of wood. It was the material for houses, ships, carts,

Viking boy using an adze

Joiners trimming planks and blocks of wood

sledges, furniture, eating-bowls—in fact for most things they used.

Trees were felled with long-handled iron felling-axes. After the branches and bark had been carefully stripped off, the logs were carefully laid criss-cross to dry and season. It was usual to leave wood to dry for several years before it was used. If it was green it would twist and split after it was carved, and that was no use at all.

When the logs were dry enough they were rough-trimmed with an adze into square blocks, or split for house walls, or else riven with mallet and wedges to make planks. Most of the wood was pine, but they also

27

Wood carver using a long-handled knife to put greater pressure on the cutting blade

used soft alder or fine ash. They used holly for small handles and delicate work in fine white wood. Oak was used where great strength and lasting qualities were needed, though it was very hard to carve because of its tough, twisted grain. They were a people who loved wood and knew all about it. When they settled in England they learned to build in stone. They used it carefully, making panels in their stone arches, and carving stone crosses with interlacing ornaments which were exactly like their woodwork.

28

Cloth Making

The most important work for the women was making cloth. They used flax and wool. Flax was plucked, and then bundled and laid to ret in water until the long clean fibres could be beaten out and combed, ready to spin into thread. Wool was clipped off the sheep with iron shears in the spring, and was then washed in wood ashes in water to get rid of the grease. Then they stroked it out with wooden combs to untangle it. It was then just like the flax, ready for spinning into thread.

The Viking women spun their thread on spindles of wood on which they had a heavy pottery bead to help keep them spinning round. This spindle was tied to some fibre and then spun quickly. Little by little the fibres twisted tight together into thread. New fibres were pulled into the growing thread from a bundle on a distaff. Women spun their thread almost all day. They spun when they were walking, and also when they

Girl combing flax fibres

Loading a shuttle with thread from a distaff

were sitting by the fire and talking indoors.

When they had enough thread they wove it into cloth. They used upright looms, in which the warp threads hung down. The warp was kept straight by pottery weights tied at the bottom. Then they wove in the weft threads with a shuttle. The cloth they made was a simple, strong material. They dyed it in various colours: black, brown, red, blue and grey. The grey homespun was the most common cloth, and every household had a stock of it. Many women had no means of dyeing their

30

cloth. Coloured cloth was mostly bought from the traders when they made their visits in the spring. It was only in rich households where there were plenty of servants that it was possible to spend much time and labour in dyeing. But all women could cut out clothes, and sew them, as well as do the mending. Most of them could also do very nice embroidery, stitched on the family clothing.

Clothes

Sometimes people would buy very fine foreign clothes from a trading ship, but mostly they made things for themselves. The men knew how to make leather shoes

A farmer
with his wife and
daughter

Winding the warp on an upright loom

and fine jewellery. The women made the cloth and made it up into clothes. The country was cold enough for people to be interested in garments that kept them warm. There were long woollen cloth stockings which were made to hitch on to a belt. Both men and women wore them, with a breech cloth in between, which was tucked into the belt at front and back. They also kept the loose stockings tidy by tying them with brightly-coloured garters just below the knees. Men sometimes cross-gartered their stockings, with long leather thongs brought up from their soft leather shoes. Women wore long linen smocks as underclothes, and in summer a linen dress, but in the winter the dress was a long woollen gown fitted in at the waist and with a full skirt, to ankle length. It had a high neck and long sleeves. For going out they had capes. In summer the cape was little more than a head-scarf, but in the cold winter they wore very long, thick woollen capes with hoods.

Men wore knee-length tunics held in with a belt. They always had a knife at their belt, and usually a sword was near, for it was a time when swords were used freely, with very little reason, in sudden quarrels. In winter they also wore long, thick woollen cloaks with hoods.

Jewellery

Everyone among the Vikings wore jewellery. There were elaborate brooches worn on the shoulder which were like big pins, with a round plate of elaborate silver and gold work, sometimes with a big jewel stone set in it. Men often wore golden rings in their ears. Women had pretty ear-rings made of gold and silver, or ivory, and sometimes of coral brought back from the distant Mediterranean Sea. Women had long and beautiful neck chains, and sometimes even imported coloured

Brooch of engraved silver

glass beads. Both sexes delighted in having fine and wide finger-rings. On their arms were bangles. For women they were delicate things, but men liked bigger rings of silver and gold, usually elaborately carved with dragons and twining plant-forms. Great chiefs had such rings to give away to any follower whom they wished to honour. It was considered a mark of a truly great man that every oarsman in his ship's crew had a golden armlet to wear.

Furs were worn almost like jewellery. They were not valued so much for softness or beauty of colour, but for the adventure of getting them. A warrior was proud to have killed a great bear, so that he could wear its skin, and perhaps make a necklace of its teeth just to warn his enemies that he was a great man. This was the whole purpose of the jewellery they wore. They wanted to show what important people they were. They liked to feel that they were as good as the best in their country. Perhaps that is why Viking period jewellery is so richly made and so much more important than most of the other things they used in life.

Family Life

Most of the Viking people loved to know all their relatives. There were always long lists of cousins, aunts and uncles to visit in the summer by ship, or, in the winter, by sledge. Father was the head of his household, and he believed that he was responsible to the gods for everyone living with him. He was in charge of all the farming and travelling. He cared for the tools and the boats. Mother was the centre of the household; she looked after the cattle, and milk and stores of grain. She was responsible

The girls help with the household work

35

for keeping the girls busy about the house cleaning and weaving. She carried the keys of the household hanging from her girdle as a sign of her importance.

Children were a happy crowd. As babies they were kept warm in a rocking-cradle, and mother sang lullabies for them. Then they would grow big enough to run about the house, and play with little copies of the things grown-ups used. There was no school for them. They learned about life on the farmstead, how to manage animals and boats, how to keep their word honourably, and how to fight. The grown-up people in the household all helped them and talked with them.

When the boys grew to be about twelve years old they were often packed off to stay with relatives to learn to be clever men. The Vikings thought it was good to mark the change in their life by a change of home. The boy had to be more independent and brave if he was away from his home for a few years.

Girls stayed with the family and learned to help with all the tasks of the household. They swept the floors with brooms of twigs and put new grass in the beds. They looked after the dairy and the malt-house where they made the bread, and, of course, they learned to spin thread and weave cloth. In a Viking farm one had to be able to do anything. There were no shops to go to for things which one could not make for daily use.

Everybody in a Viking household had plenty of work to do. Even the men, who might be sea-raiding all the summer, were busy farmers in spring and autumn. In the dark, cold winter they were wood-carving, metal-working, helping clean out the cattle byres, and, of course, making poetry.

Poetry

Poetry was very important indeed to the Vikings. It was a favourite amusement for the guests at a dinner to pass a phrase of poetry from one to the other, each making a new line to fit on to it in the correct rhythm and allitera-tion of sounds. Very few of them ever knew how to write anything except their names and some little magic charm; but they knew thousands of lines of poetry by heart.

The poems dealt with the story of the gods, and with the histories of the heroes of the past. It was always good manners to make a poem complimenting the head of the house on his bravery, and the lady of the house on her kindness. This was done to a regular pattern of words, and each line had a little pause in the middle. The two halves of the line each had the same number of syllables, and each half stressed one sound in particular.

Nothing was described by its ordinary name if there was any way to make a special descriptive name for it. These special phrases, like "The water's black raven" for a warship, were known as *kennings*, and the more of these a poet could invent for his song, the more he was praised.

Some men were naturally gifted poets. They became famous and were able to live very well, travelling from one great chief to another making poems in their praise. These skalds, as they were called, were always treated with honour and given food and fine gifts for the sweetness of their words.

Winter Life

The time for poetry and song was the dark winter. In the short hours of daylight little work could be done. It was a time when deep snow covered the ground, the hay was in the lofts, the cattle in the byres, and food all stored up. The men would go out hunting, or chopping down trees. The sap was out of the trees and the wood was drier and better for cutting at that time. In the evenings people met to eat and talk. There was a good deal of beer-drinking, but people were careful not to start quarrels in these family gatherings.

The great winter festival was Yule, when the darkest day was reached, and the great yule-log was put on the fire to bring light and warmth as a symbol of the returning sun. In the North of England Yule is now merged with Christmas, but the log is burnt, and some families, like their Viking ancestors, take a charred piece of the log and hide it under the bed to bring luck throughout the year, until it is burnt at the next Yule Festival.

After Yule there came the coldest part of the winter. In England there would be a little snow now and then, but in the homeland of the Vikings the snow was deep. People travelled on skis made of long strips of wood bound to their feet. On the trackways and on the rivers they went on sleds. Some of these sleds were beautifully carved. They were like carts mounted high up on skids

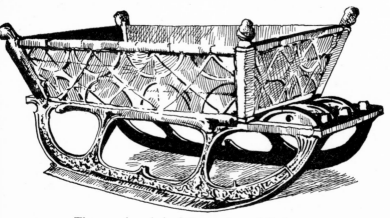

The wooden sled of Queen Asa of Oseberg

instead of wheels, and drawn by horses over the frozen rivers and lakes.

~~~~~~

Spring Time

~~~~~~

By the time the snows had gone, and frosts were ended, people were carefully watching their food supplies. Stocks were going down, and they had to rely upon a little fresh greenstuff, and fish, for living. The barrels of salt beef were empty. They would not kill any more cattle because they wanted them to breed so that there would be good fresh meat for the next winter.

It was a time of hard work, too. The land had to be broken up by the iron-shod plough. Seed had to be sown in the ploughed fields. Birds had to be scared off by the children. All life was more active now that winter was gone. They would say that the Spring Goddess Eostre was with them. Some villages would have the Spring Maiden, a pretty village girl, ride through them, like Lady Godiva, on a horse. She was a sign of growth and happiness to come.

As the days became warmer there was more time to work. Food gradually became more plentiful. Fishermen and hunters were busy. Trading-ships came in with new things to buy. Green vegetables were coming into

A two-oxen plough breaking up light soil

use. The sheep were sheared and the wool prepared for weaving.

May-time brought the flowers. There was a great festival then, and young people went out to bring in May-garlands and dance. The men were very busy getting their ships ready for voyages, and worked hard setting their houses in order. They did all the necessary repairs before the summer was upon them. Everything had to be right before summer, so that the young men of the household would be ready to go off summer-lading their ships.

Summer

In the summer the older men and the women remained at home to look after the work. There was weaving to do; cheese to make; and all the work of keeping the house in order. They watched the growing crops to keep away birds and animals which would eat the fruit and grain. They went to see their friends, and dealt with visiting traders.

Maybe the people at home would see strange black ships of raiders from the sea, sailing along the coast. If so, they would try to drive the cattle into the woods, and hide anything of value they could take with them. There was many a Viking who thought it no shame to rob and murder the families of people who were not his blood relatives.

The younger men of the family, of course, were out seeking adventure on the seas. Very few of the black ships were lone raiders. Usually groups of them would meet, and sail for adventure under some trusted nobleman. They came from farms and villages along the coast. Each crew brought their own war gear, barrels of fresh water, and big dry rings of bread for the voyage. Maybe some of them would never come home again. They might settle in some foreign land. Or maybe they

Loading a ship with bread and weapons in summer

would be killed in the battles they sought out. They fought for the fun of it, as well as for plunder. It was a great thing to be accounted a bold warrior who could frighten off his enemies, or chop them in pieces with a keen sword. He came home again with songs made about his adventures, and many a fine thing captured from other people. This 'summer-lading', as they called it, was a brave and dangerous game. One won bright gold or paid the forfeit with one's life.

43

Autumn

After the summer, with its heat and fighting, came the harvest-time. The barley and rye had to be cut by hand, with iron sickles and scythes. The straw was gathered up into racks for winter bedding for the cattle. Grass was cut and dried for hay. In the orchards there were apples to be picked; apples for eating; apples to be dried for the winter; apples for jelly; and apples for cider-brewing.

Reaping corn with a scythe

Apples and a beehive full of honey in autumn

Berries were collected in the woods for preserving as a sweetener for the dull winter diet. There was honey to be taken from the beehives and kept in store. From it they made a strong sweet mead to drink.

All that was done with the sheep in the autumn was to bring them down from the fells, and to select which should be killed and salted down for the winter. It was the same with the cattle. Good milking cows and a healthy young bullock or two were kept, but as winter drew near, the other cattle were killed and the meat either salted or smoked.

45

Autumn was a very busy time in the home. Warm winter clothes were made ready. Piles of wood for winter fuel were stacked near the house. Buckets and barrels were prepared to hold water when the streams froze over.

The round of the year was complete. The Viking family was prepared to face another quiet winter indoors. There was a little that they had bought from the traders, and not a great deal, apart from fame, won in the summer fighting. But they had enjoyed the round of the year, and were looking forward to going through it all again. It was hard work to make everything they needed themselves, but they thoroughly enjoyed doing it. In their sagas, one hears of all these activities on the farm as a background to the actions of the heroes in the story.

Ship-building

The most important possession of a Viking householder was his ship. It was his chief link with friends and relatives who lived in other parts of the country. It was his only way of seeing strange lands and winning wealth from them.

The making of a ship was a very important business. There was much prayer and asking for blessings from

Shipwrights fitting out a longship

the gods before a single piece of wood was cut. Then trees were selected for a ship. There had to be two fine, sturdy, curved pieces of oak, and lengths of nearly straight ash, several curved branches of big ash trees and a great deal of good straight pine for the ship's planks. The trees were cut in the winter, but it might be several years before the timber was used. It was packed in a cool part of the woodland, in the shade so that it would dry slowly and steadily and not crack. When it was ready the warrior would consult an expert shipwright. They would examine all the timber to see if it was fit to use. If all was well, they would begin by laying the long ash keel. It was carefully shaped with adzes. When it was ready it was rested on wooden blocks with grooves cut in them to fit it. Next the curved boughs of ash were shaped in pairs, each jointed, at the thick end, into the keel. These were the ribs of the ship. Then the oaken stem and stern posts were fitted. They had already been carved very carefully by the best wood-carver in the family. At the stem was a terrible head of a dragon, and at the stern either a dragon tail or else another smaller head. They were held in position by the broad ash gun-wales of the ship which ran on either side from stem to stern. Each rib was jointed into its proper place on the gunwales too. At this stage the Viking ship was a skeleton with strong oak fore and aft, and all the framework in between made of strong but springy ash. It was ideal for the rough seas through which it would have to sail.

The Ship's Hull

The posts were specially cut to take the ends of the pine boards which made up the hull. The boards were laid in position and fixed by big wooden pegs and iron rivets to the ribs. The ship was clinker-built: that is, the edges of the boards overlapped a little at the joints. They were not smoothed off outside like most modern boats.

When the ship was completed, she was about sixty feet long, and amidships her beam was about twelve to fifteen feet. Her hull was about five feet deep. At either end the stem and stern came up to nearly the height of a man above her sides. Across the ribs wooden planks were fixed as seats for the rowers, and fore and aft were small decks for the look-out and the steersman. In the centre a strong bench with a heavy wooden framing took the twenty-foot-high mast with its long cross spar from which the sail would hang. It was fitted up with ropes so that the spar could be raised or lowered;

Tarring a completed ship, to make her watertight

49

D

and, if needed, the mast itself could be taken down.

The ship was next caulked with flax fibres and dry moss, driven tight with wooden mallets, so that every joint between her planks was made tight and safe against water. Then she was painted with thick, black pine tar. This was made by roasting pine-logs over a slow fire and scraping off the resin as it oozed out of them. It was melted again in an iron cauldron over a big fire near the ship, and pasted on her timbers with fibre brooms. After this the dragons were painted and gilded, and she was ready for the water.

Launching the Ship

She was taken down from her cradle and run on rollers into the sea. When it was seen that she was floating just right, she was trimmed with a ballast of large stones put in her bilges. Then the crew hoisted the striped linen sail on its long yard, and she was ready for fitting out for her first voyage.

First came the steering paddle, a great paddle some twelve feet or more in length, with a blade two feet wide. This was lashed over her stern and served as a rudder. Then came the long oars of ash, anything from ten to twenty pairs, according to the size of the ship. They were held in flexible leather tholes between two wooden pins, which took the place of modern rowlocks. Her anchor was a rock tied to a rope. She was beautiful, a hand-made ship, graceful and dark, and consecrated to the gods of the Vikings.

As she floated near the beach her crew came aboard, wading with their tunics rolled round their waists, and hose and armour bundled on their backs. They swung into her, and dressed. Then small boats with water barrels, food, and with loads of spears, arrows and axes came alongside her, and she was ready. Carved wood shields, coloured red and blue, were fixed on her sides to show that she was a war vessel. The steersman was ready; the wind was right; the Captain stood ready in polished helmet and hauberk. The word was given to sail. So many a brave Thane and Jarl went on their ships, new built for adventure.

Navigation

The Vikings had no compasses to guide their ships across the sea. Yet they made long voyages out of sight of land. The longest we know was that of Thorfinn Karlsefni who decided to visit his relatives in Greenland. He took his ship from Norway right across the sea without touching at Iceland, and sailed into South Greenland successfully. They all knew how to sail by the stars at night. If you kept the Pole Star over your right shoulder you were going westwards, and if it was over your left shoulder you were going eastwards. By day, the position of the sun, at mid-day and sunrise or sunset, helped a lot. This would have been all very well if they rowed all the way, but that would have been too much hard work for humans to stand. The Vikings relied on sailing before the wind most of the time. Their secret was a knowledge of the ways of the winds in the Atlantic. If you sailed from the mouth of the Baltic Sea on a south wind, the odds were that before very long it would change to south-east, and then to east. When the wind changed to north-east it was time to shorten sail and row for a time. After that you could expect the cycle of winds to start up all over again.

They knew well enough that this was right north of the British Isles, and wrong south of them; so their Atlantic sailing was usually done well to the north. It was a good thing for them that they made the long voyages in summer time.

Nearer England they preferred to go round by the Atlantic coasts, because in the North Sea and the narrow English Channel the tides were higher and the currents much stronger. On the western side they could

52

reckon on south-west winds and the northerly drift of the Gulf Stream. It was never an easy journey, but on the west the conditions were much more steady. That is why so many Viking raids came round Manchester, and up the Bristol Channel, or on to the Dorset coasts.

Sea Fights

When the black ships came to strange coasts they would seek a place to land. The Captain would release two ravens. They were sacred to Odin. One would circle and one fly forwards. They followed the forward-flying bird.

There was once a Captain who did not believe in Odin. He killed a raven and nailed its wings to his helmet. Soon he was destroyed in battle and other Viking warriors sung about the evil fate which befell men with wings on their helmets.

The very fact that the black ships turned towards the land was a signal for the people on shore to get away.

A Viking warrior in battle

But often enough brave men would man ships and come out to fight the raiders. The ships would be rowed towards each other. Archers in the rigging would shoot at the crews. Warriors in their narrow helmets and long war-coats would be on the platforms at stem and stern. Some of them carried heavy spears to cast at the ship, and if possible hole her. The favourite plan was to try to get very close to the stern of the enemy so as to board her. A few brave men with swords and shields would start the fight. The crew would swing boarding-axes to pull in the other ship by her gunwale. Then up they

A longship with dragon prow sailing to battle

Grappling the enemy with boarding-axes

went, over the sides, pushing their shields into the faces of the enemy and slicing with their axes. Maybe they would spare a few of the enemy crew, but they usually preferred to kill them all. Then they would take away anything valuable in the ship, and sink her.

The only device which ever defeated a serious Viking raid at sea was the heightened walls of the ships designed by King Alfred of England. Alas! He had too few of them. Being taller than the raiders, their crew could pick off the Viking warriors with arrows before leaping down to the hand-to-hand struggle.

Battles on the Land

The raiders were not usually caught at sea. They would run their ships up the beach, leap overboard and pull them up to safety from the tide. Then they would line up together. These tall men with long golden moustaches, helmets down to their eyes and long coats covered with iron rings or small iron plates, must have looked very terrifying. They had round shields, and grim, long-handled axes with a point on the lower end of the blade.

At their sides were swords about thirty inches long. Their feet and legs were cased in thick leather shoes and hose. In the middle of the group would be the symbol of the black raven with its wings spread. This was more than a banner; it was a threat that the ravens would soon fly to eat the bodies of the people slain by the Vikings.

Part of the Viking practice was to frighten people by cruelty. They would kill everybody they caught: men, women and children. One of them was jokingly called ''The Children's Friend'', because he was the first great warrior to stop his men tossing babies on the points of their spears. When raiding, there was no law for the other side. Homes were burnt and anything valuable plundered.

They thought Christianity was a crazy religion which

made people weak. They could never understand why monks prayed instead of fighting. So they often caught them and tortured them just for fun. In south-east London a Viking army killed the Bishop because he would not eat meat. They beat him to death with beef bones from their butcher's slaughter-house. That was near Lesnes Abbey, not far from Woolwich.

In the end the bravest of them all, King Olaf Trygvasson, became a Christian and fought the wild Vikings until they accepted his rule and his religion. You can read the strange story in the Saga of King Olaf, which

Viking war leaders with the Raven Standard

the American poet, Longfellow, translated into English. Olaf, too, started an English song, ''London Bridge is Falling Down''. His was the long ship which put ropes round the piles of the wooden London Bridge in Saxon times; and his crew rowed hard until the bridge was broken down.

In Iceland the Viking settlers held a parliament (called a *Thing*) and voted that their country should become Christian in the year 1000. They had discovered that there was more good progress made by Christian people than by the old heathen. So the wooden images were burnt, and the new religion accepted.

The Old Gods

The Vikings of the old days believed in a famous group of gods who were like the gods of the Anglo-Saxons. There was Odin All-Father, who was a King of Heaven, Thor Redbeard the Storm God, Frigg, wife of Odin, Freya, Lady of the Spring, Loki the Spirit of Evil, Tiw the God of War, and Saeter the underworld god. There were many others, and among them the great giants and strange dwarfs, all of whom represented the powers of nature. Most of the Viking gods had once been heroes on earth and were the founders of Royal Families.

People knew of ancient burial mounds in Sweden which they said were the graves of Thor and Odin.

Although these gods ruled the natural world where the Vikings lived, there was a general belief that one day the gods would be overthrown, and a new religion come to mankind, in which only a few of the ancient gods would survive. They said that long ago Odin had bound the Wolf Fenris and his mother in a deep cavern. He did this by trickery. The wise men knew that one day the Wolf would break free and devour the sun. In the end he would destroy Valhalla, where the gods and heroes lived in the heavens.

The Vikings believed that the rainbow was the bridge by which the souls of brave warriors slain in battle rode up to the halls of Odin. There in happiness they would feast and drink for ever—or at least until the day Ragnarok, when all would be destroyed. It was a brave, somewhat savage religion, but in the end even great Odin would be subject to justice because of his crime against the Wolf.

Law and Justice

The Vikings believed that every man should answer for his family's actions. Responsibility was laid on the heads of families. If the son of a farmer stole something from another farmhouse, the father was bound to pay the damages. It was nobody's business how he made his son pay back.

Because they were a scattered people, it was not easy to deal with lawsuits at once. People concerned in a serious affair, such as murder, were bound to tell their neighbours that there was a dangerous quarrel. Then they let the whole matter drop until the next meeting of the *Thing*. This was a gathering to which all the head men of all the families of a district went to deal with lawsuits. If people tried to take revenge for a crime on their own, they risked being made outlaws. It was very bad to be outlawed, because anybody had the right to kill or rob an outlaw without paying compensation.

At the *Thing* people who were concerned in a serious quarrel came in person. Often they brought numbers of friends with them. All carried their swords because they were free men. At the *Thing* a Lawgiver, who was well known as an honest and wise man, was appointed. The people concerned in the dispute would ask clever friends to speak for them. The whole case was brought forward step by step, so that the Lawgiver would know every little detail. At the end of the smaller cases he would give his judgment, and say how much was to be paid to the person who had been wronged. But in very serious cases he would call a few older men whom he knew to be

Disputing a case before the Lawgiver at the Thing

friends of the people concerned in the case. They would then agree among themselves what it was best to do, and who should pay the fine. Of course the rulings at the *Thing* were usually obeyed. Any householder could refuse to accept them; but that usually meant he must be prepared to be an outlaw and fight his way to escape to some distant land. Later he was allowed to return to another *Thing* and plead his case once again.

Kings and Chiefs

The Vikings loved their personal freedom so much that they found it very hard to be subject to their kings.

Kings ruled because they were closer in descent to Odin than other chiefs. They had also to be brave and clever men who could avoid quarrels with their more powerful followers, and assure peace in the land over which they ruled. The Vikings thought a really great king was a clever war leader, and a very generous man who gave gifts of gold. Around him were a group of *Thanes*, noblemen who would do no common work, but earned their living by war, and as leaders of armies. They were pledged to defend the king with their lives, and to fight for him in his battles. In return he gave them rights to land and gifts of food, fine clothes, wonderful weapons, and gold. To these young braves the King was the Giver of Gold, and the Fountain of Honour. Other important men were the *Jarls*, who were like lesser kings on their own. They owned land and were overlords of many farmers. They led their own warships in the service of the king. In a free and independent way they promised to serve him, and to pay him homage and give him tribute as their overlord.

Sometimes an independent Viking might be made a nobleman because of his fame as a raider and winner of wealth. If he had won much gold and silver he would give away his treasures to persuade other Vikings to come with him. With any luck he could form a powerful private army and fight his way to an Earldom overseas in England or Normandy. Sometimes the kings managed to bring such brave men into their service by gifts of land and servants, in return for the oath which bound them to serve and protect their overlord, the King.

Freemen and Serfs

Beneath the nobles came the landowners and small farmers. They had the full protection of the law; being free men, they farmed or went raiding just as they wished. Usually they preferred to band together or join

one of the noblemen in a big raid, but they never felt bound to serve in that way if they did not wish to do so. Most of them had servants about the farm who were also free. These men were only farm hands who could never rank as warriors. The warriors expected them to run away in a fight, but used them to do the hard work on the farm. They were the ploughmen, tanners, labourers

A free farm servant   and the like.

63

A few people were bondsmen. They were true serfs, bound to their masters, with little hope of any freedom. They were treated almost like animals, and had practically no rights in law. The fine for killing one of them was so small that it was hardly worth receiving. Sometimes a freeman sold himself and his family into serfdom. This often happened in times of famine when they could get food only from some powerful landowner on such cruel terms. Others became serfs by the judgment of the courts. There was no prison to which offenders could be sent. In some cases the only way in which compensation for a crime could be paid was work for the person who had been injured.

Tradesmen

Among the Vikings every man was prepared to do a great deal of work which we should leave to be done by a skilled workman. But in the small towns, which formed around the best harbours, or where the more important nobles lived, there were a few specialist tradesmen. They made fine things which great people liked to have in their possession.

Skilled carvers worked in ivory. Ivory came from the narwhal, and also from walrus tusks. The best ivory

Armlets of silver and gold

came from Iceland and Greenland. Traders brought it back in exchange for clothes and metal work which they sold to the settlers. Maybe the ivory carvers would buy it with gold coin, but they might also exchange their finished work for the raw material. A fine ivory chess set was worth several tusks to the trader. Or maybe a lady would wish for some ivory ornaments and pay for them in silver or cloth embroidered by her hand-maidens. To carve ivory needed a great deal of care and patience. The knives used were made of hard steel, and the carver must not let his hand slip while he worked. A small scratch would spoil the beautiful surface of the creamy ivory.

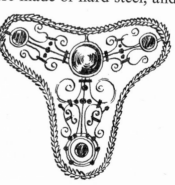

Workers in gold and silver preferred to hammer and carve their metal rather than melt and cast it. They

An engraved brooch

65

E

A drinking horn of glass, imported from the Rhineland

made armlets and brooches with such complex designs that it was easier to cast the rough shape, or hammer it out if it was a solid form, and then engrave the design on it afterwards. After that they worked with punch, chisel and graving-tool to shape it as they wished. Most of them were able to set their jewellery with garnets, and some workmen were able to do some enamel work. This meant filling spaces in the metal-work with powdered coloured glass. Then the work was heated until the glass melted and filled the space with colour.

Merchants

A merchant was as much a fighting man as any warrior, so he was respected in Viking society. His ship was broader and slower than the warship, and it had covered spaces for delicate cargo. Some of the goods were covered with tarpaulins, large sheets of cloth painted thick with pine-tar to keep water out. On the trading ships there were always shields ready to hang on the gunwales if they were attacked by sea-rovers. The crew always carried armour and weapons with them.

The merchant ship would most often set out with a cargo of skins, amber, ivory, dried fish, and other Northern goods. These would be taken south and exchanged against gold coin, or fine cloths, pottery and jewellery. Many a trading voyage lasted two or three years. Viking merchants would travel along all the coasts of Northern Europe, and even venture past the

Crew unloading a merchant ship

Trader selling fine cloth from the Mediterranean

Arab fortresses in the Mediterranean to visit Italy and Greece. The risks were great because the Arab sea-rovers were as fierce as the Vikings; but the gain was great. If all went well, they would go home again with corals, pearls, and oriental silks bought in Constantinople.

Most merchant-ships were content to visit the coasts of Britain and Germany, trading in cloth and metal-work. They took out furs and came back with gold and silver coins, glass vessels and enamelwork. There was also the Northern trade. Ships would go off to Iceland and even Greenland in search of ivory, white bear skins, sealskins and, above all, ermine skins. The journeys were dangerous enough in those stormy waters, but they brought great profits. The outward cargo was usually of fine cloth, good timber, and spices: all things which the Northern settlers could not produce themselves. The settlers thought it a wonderful bargain to obtain a fine blue cloth tunic in return for a pair of ivory tusks from a walrus. After all, they could find plenty of walrus to hunt whenever they had time.

So, in one way or another, the merchants spread goods around the world from Greenland to Constantinople. In those wild times it was a dangerous calling. The merchant was really an adventurer, and risked his life and cargo on every voyage.

Fishermen

Some merchants traded dried fish from the North to Britain and France; but most Viking farmers were also fishermen. The cold seas have always been the best fishing-grounds in the world. They teemed with herring, haddock, cod and hake. A man who had a boat need never starve in those days.

There were many ways of fishing: with rod and line, with nets from a single boat, and with a seine net trailed between two boats. It was not necessary to go far from land in order to get a good catch, especially off the steep shores of the Norwegian fjords. Fishers used quite small boats rowed by only one or two men. They always watched the weather so that they should not be caught up in sudden storms or lost in evening fog. They knew what fish to expect in different months, and whether they would be swimming in shoals up or down the coast.

There was a lot of inland fishing too. Many a boy learnt how to slip his hand into a stream and snatch out a fat trout. It took real skill to do that. The reward was a very nice dinner. There were also special seasons when the eels came down the rivers by the million on their way to the sea. Then each farm would set its eel traps, plaited from osier twigs, to catch a supply. In the other direction salmon came up stream each year. As they swarmed in silver shoals up the rivers they would be netted, or caught with salmon gaffs. Those were rich days indeed. Fine salmon were caught in the Thames by London Bridge. In the North of England, among the Viking settlers by the Tyne, Tees and Humber, the fishing was almost as rich as in the old homeland.

Fish-Curing

In the spring people expected to live on fish because all

the meat had been eaten up. At other times they preferred to have different food. All the same, they caught
far more fish than could ever be eaten fresh. The prob-
lem was solved by smoke-drying and salting it. Whenever there was a storm or when the winter made fishing
too difficult, each household had a good reserve of dried
fish to keep them alive and well-fed. When smoking fish,
it was usual to make a hut of upright poles which supported racks inside. From the racks hundreds of fish
were hung. They had already been cleaned out, and split
open. They were held open by wooden skewers, and

Smoking the fish for the winter store

hung up on thin wooden rods passed through the heads. Underneath them a fire was lit. It was choked down by sawdust and wood chips so that it kept smoking and smouldering. The smoke warmed and dried the fish slowly. It penetrated right into them, so that they became a dry brownish yellow and would keep for months without going bad. Different kinds of wood-smoke gave different flavours, but most people preferred the sharp flavour given by oak sawdust.

Salmon turned a dark pink when they were smoked, and of course they were a favourite fish for special occasions. An oil was pressed out from salmon liver which was pleasanter to drink than that from cod. Fish oil was drunk and the people knew that it was good for their health. It was also used for greasing leather, where the smell did not matter.

Stockfish were split and smoked like the salmon, but they turned yellow, like the small cod and hake and big herrings. When they were smoked they were usually packed in barrels. At the bottom of the barrel was a layer of coarse sea salt. Between each layer of fish more salt was laid down. Such fish would last for years. Before they were used they had to be soaked in several changes of water, otherwise they would be much too salty to eat.

Meat was smoked over fires too, but this was done for

the hunters who would take a supply of dried meat with them as food for their journey. It was useful because it could be eaten without cooking; so no fire need be lit to frighten the game.

Hunting

A hunt on land was a great sport for the Vikings. They did not depend on it for their food, but it brought in pleasant kinds of meat they would not have enjoyed

Hunting a wild boar

otherwise. The best hunting was reserved for men who owned horses: that is to say, for men of noble family. The farm-hands and serfs were expected to beat the game out of cover or bring the dogs on foot. Little boys, of course, caught small animals for fun.

Sometimes a party of free farmers would combine to hunt deer in the forests. It needed skill to either tire out or head off the animal. When at last it had been cornered and killed, by a knife-thrust across its throat, there was a joyful procession home to divide up the good venison for dinner.

Much more dangerous animals for the braver warrior-hunters to tackle were bears and boars. The wild boar and his family would raid the farms in the spring and root up the crops. If people tried to drive them off, they might easily turn on them and kill them. The sharp tusks of a wild boar could tear one like a knife. So when these dangerous animals came out of the forest, hunting parties of the brave young men were formed. This dangerous game of boar-hunting was thought to be a proper sport for noblemen.

Dogs were used to scent the trail of the boar and lead the hunters to him. The hunters were mounted and armed with spears. They followed the dogs. Usually the boar would trot as fast as a dog could run until it found a corner to stand at bay. As the dogs rushed at it, it would swing its head and hurl them into the air, ripped open by its sharp tusks. The hunters would circle and seek for a chance of spearing the massive animal. But there was always the chance that the boar would rush at them from the left side and lame the horse and perhaps rip up the leg of the rider. If the rider came off, he was likely to be killed before his friends could help him. However, a brave hunter would face these dangers and try to spear the boar just behind the shoulder while the dogs were keeping it busy. Some very brave men would hunt the boar on foot and try to spear its throat as it charged them. But a full-grown and active boar weighed twice as much as a man, so it was a dangerous game even if the boar were speared at the first thrust. After the hunt the boar's tusks were taken by the killer.

More than one brave Viking wore a helmet covered with boar tusks. They not only kept off sword blows as well as iron would, but they were also a trophy of which any warrior might be proud.

Bear-hunting was less dangerous, but Bruin was a cautious and clever foe and often knocked down his hunters before he was cornered. The Vikings liked bear meat, and bear fat was splendid stuff for softening and waterproofing leather. It was also good for the hair. The real danger of bears was that one might meet them when one was alone on a forest trail. There is a story of a young man who was on a bear hunt. He slipped as the bear came at him, and his companions ran away. It was on the rocky edge of a fjord. He gripped the bear and threw it over the cliff, knowing well that he could not escape, but that the bear, being bigger and heavier, would come down on the rocks first. It did. When he came back home, all his companions were afraid it was his ghost, until he showed them the bear's foot which he had cut off.

Ghosts

The Vikings were afraid of ghosts. Sometimes their relatives who had died would appear in dreams to warn them of danger. They could understand that well enough. But a white shape in the dark would frighten all but the bravest. Their stories were full of ghosts and bogies. Sometimes the ghosts were powerful monsters who would shake a house to pieces, or devour sleeping warriors. At other times they would tempt men to fall over cliffs or into rivers.

When someone in the family died, they did all they could to prevent the ghost coming back to frighten them. Dead bodies were taken out through a hole in the side of the house and not through the door. People would try to disguise themselves by putting on old, blackened clothes and letting their hair and beards grow untidy. The body was hurried away to burial, feet first. It must not know the way back. Then it was buried deep and soft in a moss-lined grave. This is not to say that the Vikings were glad to get rid of dead relatives. It was with deep sorrow that they prayed the gods to lead their loved ones over the rainbow bridge to Heaven. But they were really afraid of ghosts. They felt that only something very wrong in their fate would draw a ghost back to earth. Otherwise it might be an evil spirit, and better avoided.

Great warriors and kings were given a ship burial. They were put in a ship with their treasures. Sometimes it was burnt, but more often the whole splendid monument was covered by a great mound of earth called a *howe*. Queen Asa was buried in such a *howe* at Gokstad. Her grave was excavated some years ago. There were jewels there, and also the best preserved Viking ship we know. The Queen's chair, bedstead, and her sled for travelling on the ice were all preserved in the tomb. So beautiful was the woodwork that we gained a new understanding of the Vikings as a cultured and civilised people.

The Vikings would have been very surprised that we did not find a dragon in the *howe*, or that the dead queen was not there sitting in her chair to speak to the people

77

who came to rob her of her treasures. Their heroic stories often brought in such eerie episodes. As a matter of fact, many of their heroes did go alone to find the graves of their famous forefathers. If they were fortunate they might find a treasure, of which the most important thing would be the famous sword used by the dead man. They would ask for the sword and believe that their ancestor allowed them to find it, so that they, in turn, could do great deeds with it. Such a hero's sword had its personal name and was treated as if it were a living person. It was respected by its owner as a sign of his bravery, and feared by all his enemies, who would often keep away rather than face such a famous weapon.

Viking Children

In Viking days the whole world seemed full of stories of heroes and gods, and of everyday life on the farms. Once a baby was running around and beginning to talk, mother and the other children started to tell him the old Saga stories. Growing boys and girls wanted to be like their favourite characters in the Sagas. The girls would like to be Gudrun, wise wife of Sigurd Dragon-Slayer, even if they did lose their husbands in battle. Was it not better to marry a hero and nurse his babies, than to be the drab little wife of a poor farmer who always ran away from his enemies? And the boys, too, would think of the great warriors whom they admired. Would they be fierce and very strong like Grettir the Icelander, or clever poets and brave fighters like Kormak the Skald? They did not dream of wives; they wanted just to be brave and wise warriors.

A Viking boy

There was no school to tie them down to the routine of lessons. Girls learnt from the women of the household and boys from the men. They were up at sunrise and went to bed at sunset. How they managed to sleep when the grown-ups were talking and singing in the great wooden hall beside their bedrooms is quite a puzzle.

Small children just ran about the household. They got in the way of the grown-ups and were rolled on one side, or they were picked up and petted, but they were never neglected. People liked to watch their children and see if they could guess what kind of men and women they would be when fully grown up. Even when they got into

Playing fivestones on the shore of the Vik

mischief there was always a laugh and the remark that they were getting like old so-and-so who used to do just that kind of thing when he was young.

They played many of the games that we know. "Poor Jenny is a weeping", and "In and Out the Houses" were enjoyed by the girls and smaller children. The boys played at horses, and had mock battles and tug-of-war. There was hop-scotch, and races, and of course target practice with bow and arrow and spears: wooden ones, of course! All boys wrestled, and loved wrestling as a sport. There were strict rules to be followed, as in all sports. Indoors they played with soft leather balls stuffed with feathers. They never saw a rubber ball, for in those days there was no rubber in Europe. There were plenty of games with marbles, and five-stones. "Cat's cradle" was played with lengths of string, and there were lots of guessing games like "Tip-it". They also played chess and dominoes, and threw dice for gambling. In the long winter evenings the grown-ups joined in the games too, and taught the youngsters how to play more cunningly.

When the boys began to be big fellows of eleven or so, they were sent off to stay with relatives. They learned to work about the house, to do some wood carving, and to handle weapons. They soon learned to hunt, but all the time they were learning how to be brave and active so that they could become good warriors.

If the boys had quick minds they learned how to make up clever poems, and also how to keep reckonings on the farm. The reckonings were kept on squared blocks of wood. On each of the four edges numbers were cut by making notches. There would be one reckoning staff for sheep and one for cows, and others for lengths of cloth, or numbers of smoked hams, and so on. There was always one special wooden almanac for keeping a reckoning of the days of the year so that people would know on which day to rest, and which

F

was a festival of the gods. It was something which every boy was expected to know, because one day he might become head of a household.

Girls also were expected to keep a reckoning of what was in the household. When they grew up they would be responsible for all the things inside the house, just as their husbands would have to look after all business outside.

All young people bothered a great deal about their appearance. Boys wanted to wear fine manly tunics, and girls prided themselves upon their neat, clean clothes. Boys and girls wore their hair long. The boys brushed and combed their hair loose, and the girls wore theirs in long plaits tied with pretty ribbons which they wove themselves.

When they were big enough, they waited on their elders at table. The boys brought in the meat, and the girls poured out the honey-mead or barley-beer as they were asked. In that way they learned good table manners.

Marriage

Among the Vikings people married quite young. A boy might well be a famous warrior by the time he was eighteen, and well able to marry and keep a good home.

A Viking wedding feast

Girls married a little younger, round about sixteen. It was usual for young people to drop a hint to their parents about whom they would like to marry. Usually the young man would persuade an aunt to call on the girl's parents to ask if she would be free to marry him. If all seemed right, the heads of the two families would meet to discuss the whole business. They had to arrange what presents were to be exchanged between the families, and how many relatives on each side were to come to the wedding feast. A house and furniture had to be provided for the young couple. It was quite a business. But the girl always had the final word. She had the right to accept her future husband, or else to say she would have nothing to do with him. Her decision was the important thing. All the other arrangements depended upon her choice.

There were two sides to the marriage: the social arrangement between the families, and the personal marriage before the gods. Long before the days when the Vikings accepted Christianity, they exchanged wedding rings as a pledge of faith between them. They promised to live together in peace and to share all their goods. The husband was expected to defend his wife with his sword, the wife to spin cloth for her husband's clothes from the wool on her distaff.

After the wedding there was great feasting, and many guests came, bringing gifts of fine jewellery and clothing. The bride and bridegroom, for the first time in their lives, sat on the high seats at the head of the table. They were expected to have kind words for everyone and see that their guests ate and drank all they could. They were not to eat or drink very much themselves. People watched all the time for lucky or unlucky signs, so that they would guess how the marriage would go. But, since the bride and bridegroom were soon the only sober people at the party, they did not worry much. They were much more concerned to see that no quarrels broke out at the feast. When it was over, they made sure that the guests were comfortably wrapped up where they slept on the benches around the hall.

After the wedding the young couple settled down to the hard everyday tasks of their farm. To us all this hard work from dawn to dusk for both men and women would be killing. But when we read the old Sagas we find no grumbling. The Viking people knew of no easier way of life. As they worked they found time to sing and talk. Life was always interesting, and they rarely complained. In those days they died younger than we do, but life was very full for them.

Apart from wars the men were the farmers, builders, and carvers. The women were cooks and cleaners, the preservers of the food and the makers of cloth.

Dyeing Cloth

Among the most interesting things a woman could do was to dye her wool and linen. Not all the farmers' wives knew the art of colouring cloth. Those who could do it well were able to make a good living by dyeing cloth for the whole neighbourhood.

The yarn or cloth had to be carefully cleaned before dyeing. It was often boiled in a lye of finely-sifted wood-ash in water. This removed the grease. Then it was dipped in a bath of hot dye and soaked until the dye liquid had spread evenly through every fibre. It was very important to do this quite thoroughly; otherwise the colour might come out patchy and nasty to look at. The cloth was next taken to another bath and fixed by boiling up with wood-ash lye, or else with salt crystals, which fixed the dyestuff in the fibre of the cloth, and helped to prevent it from fading or washing out later on. After this came a final rinsing. Then the cloth was dried and made ready for use.

Nearly every house could make the grey cloth which came from woollen cloth washed in a simple lye. In effect it was unbleached wool. But those who knew the dye-plants could do much better. A soft reddish-brown was made from the madder plant. Ferns and onions helped to make light brown. There was a golden colour made from a kind of lichen. The Irish people traded their saffron dye made from the bulbs of autumn crocus. There was a scarlet dye, much valued, made from a rare fungus, and black ink-like dyes made from oak gall. The famous blue cloth, so much valued by people of good family, was dyed with woad. Woad dyeing was an unpleasant process. The plant had to be mashed and left in pits to ferment. It had a nasty smell, except to the dyers who knew it was going to bring them a good living. The dye liquid was nearly clear, and the colour came out only in the second bath where the cloth was boiled in lye. When it did appear, it was beautiful: a soft grey-blue which was very handsome in the deeper shades.

The bright clothes which came from the dyers were festival garments. They were worn by farmer families on great occasions. Of course nobles and warriors always wore fine clothes, just to show how important they were.

Music and Dancing

Singing was an everyday part of life in Viking times. Work was always easier when one had a song. The sailors had their shanties to keep time in rowing. There were wood-cutters' songs, weaving songs, songs for sheep-shearing, and lullabies for baby's sleep. You have probably heard some of those old songs from the Hebrides, where there were more Viking people than Scottish in the old times. All the same many a Viking family had learnt the songs of the Celtic people, as well as their own.

At festivals there were plenty of special songs and ballads. The skalds always went with a small harp under their arms, ready to sing their poetry, or play a few notes in a pattern of sound as they recited. King Alfred

Bringing in the May garlands

took such a small harp with him when he went disguised as a skald into the camp of the Danish invaders in Somerset.

The little harp was not loud enough for dances. There was kettledrum and fife, and in some places a kind of simple bagpipe. Most people sang when they danced. The dances were rather like our folk-dances, with groups of people skipping and gliding into the figures. They were all singing and thoroughly enjoying it. They might attempt a sword-dance at a festival; but usually

88

skilled people did that, and frightened the company by dancing with bare feet, in and out of sharp swords lying edge-upwards on the floor.

Warriors had special dances which survive today in some of our North-country sword-dances. In these the men swing their swords into patterns of threes and fives and so on, each time interweaving the blades into stars. At the end they formed a star around one of the dancers in the middle of the ring, so that it looked as if they were dancing with his head on a star-shaped dish of steel. It is still quite frightening when done with tin swords. It must have looked much fiercer when these tall, fair warriors danced with sharp, steel swords and slowly circled with a head in the centre of the ring. It was still more frightening in war when a row of them slowly marched forward singing a rhythmic chant as they swung their swords and lifted their shields in time, all the while with their blue eyes staring steadily under the brims of their bright helmets. Song and dance were not always just for fun among the Vikings.

The Kings Conquer

The Vikings took to raiding more than ever before when King Harald seized control of all Norway in 872.

Gradually the discontented Viking chiefs went away or surrendered to the kings. The end of Viking days came when the great Danish King Cnut (or Canute as the English called him) established control over Denmark and England. The sea-rovers were cooped up in the North, and those who had ventured into Britain and France were separated. Canute, at first by battle, and then by clever political bargaining, brought peace to England for his life-time at least. He left the Vikings in Normandy to find their own way. In Norway and Sweden his power helped the kings to win final control. Only in Iceland did the Vikings keep their old freedom; but that was mostly because they kept order and peace amongst themselves. They made wise laws in the first of all parliaments, and kept faithfully to them.

The Icelanders voted to be Christians. Most other Vikings followed their Kings and accepted the White Christ. It was then that they first learnt to control themselves. To win battles was no longer enough. They found that there was something good in being merciful to conquered people. They learned that the slaying of men was not the best way to ride the rainbow Bridge to Heaven. From the timid monks they learned how to read and write. Before long they were able to write down the stories told by their skalds, and preserve the heroic tales of the olden times for us to read.

What the Vikings have given us

We may never read the Sagas of the old times, but most of us have played Viking games, and sung Viking songs at school without knowing it. Remember "In and Out the Windows", and "Walney Echoes, One, Two, Three"? Maybe we have seen sword-dancers doing the old traditional dances. Many of our words and place-names, like Whitby, Skegness and Thorpe, come from the Viking times. We may go and see the earthen mounds and ditches of some Viking camp, or perhaps visit an old church like that at Earls Barton in Northamptonshire, which was made by Christians in the days when the Vikings were newly converted. As a nation, we have many of the ways of the Vikings among our ancestors. They loved travel and adventure; they faced danger without any fuss, and they loved to sing whenever they found work was boring.

Above all things, the Vikings loved their personal freedom. The old and true saying, that "An Englishman's home is his castle", exactly reflects the Viking spirit. No one was welcome in a Viking homestead, be he king or slave, unless he came in peace and friendship at the invitation of his host. From that love of freedom came the idea of holding the "*Thing*" where they made their own laws, and settled their quarrels. These Viking gatherings of free householders were the real beginning of our way of governing ourselves through an elected Parliament.

Our old Viking ancestors were not very civilised, but if it had not been for their brave way of life, and their love of freedom, we should not have had much chance of becoming really civilised ourselves.